Contents

An apple is a fruit

Apples are a kind of fruit. They are sweet and crunchy to eat.

Apples can be red, green or yellow.

I Know That!

ples

ewellyn

HAV

W
FRANKLIN WATTS

First published in 2005 by Franklin Watts
338 Euston Road
London
NW1 3BH

Franklin Watts Australia
Level 17/207 Kent Street, Sydney NSW 2000

Series advisor: Gill Matthews, non-fiction literacy specialist
and Inset trainer
Editor: Caryn Jenner
Series design: Peter Scoulding
Designer: James Marks
Photography: Ray Moller unless otherwise credited
Acknowledgements:Nigel Cattlin/Holt Studios: 11, 13c, 13br. Copella Fruit Juices: 18. Peter Currell/
Ecoscene: 17. Pierre Gleizes/Still Pictures: 15. Willem Harinck/Holt Studios: 16. James Marks: 1, 10b,
14. Sally Morgan/Ecoscene: 5br. Norman Rout/Ecoscene: 12b, 23t. Inga Spence/Holt Studios: 22b.
Thanks to our models: Freddy Marks, Casey Liu, Jakob Hawker, Reanne Birch

A CIP catalogue record for this book is available from the British Library

ISBN: 978 0 7496 8892 9

Printed in Malaysia

Franklin Watts is a division of Hachette Children's Books, an Hachette UK company.
www.hachettelivre.co.uk

▼ *Most of us eat apples.*

What kind of
apples do you
like best?

▼ *Wasps eat apples,
too. So do many
other animals.*

5

Apples are good for us

Apples are good for our bodies. Some people eat an apple every day to help them stay healthy.

▶ *Apples give us energy.*

6

Fruit is good for us.

What other fruits do you like to eat?

Looking at an apple

An apple has different parts.

▶ On the outside of an apple are the stalk and the peel.

Stalk

Peel

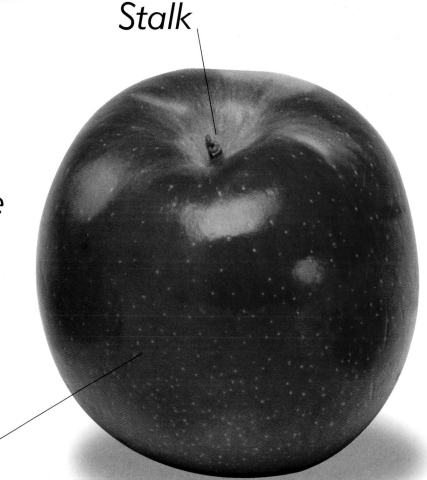

8

Inside are the flesh, the core and the seeds.

Try planting apple seeds in a pot of compost. Keep the compost damp. In a few weeks, the seeds should start to grow.

Seeds

Flesh

Core

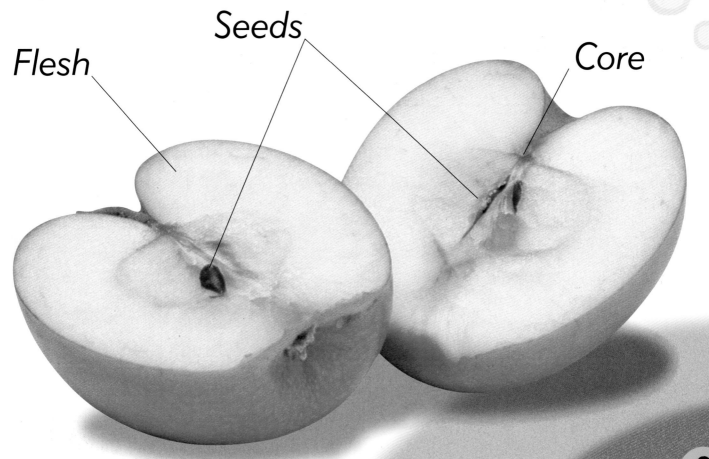

Apples grow on trees

Apples are the fruit of the apple tree.

▶ *This apple tree is growing in a garden.*

These apple trees are growing on a farm.

Many fruit farms grow apples. The trees are planted in big fields called orchards.

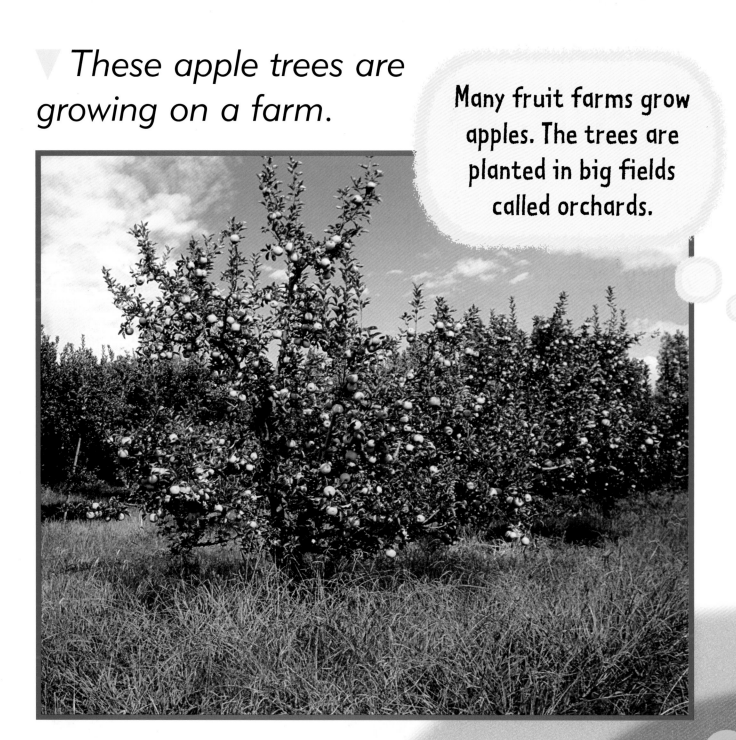

Apple blossom

In spring, apple trees
grow flowers called blossom.

▶ *Blossom
stays on the
apple tree
for two or
three weeks.*

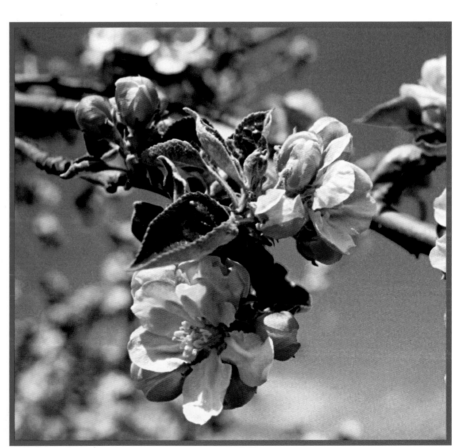

Then tiny apples begin to grow on the tree.

In the blossom is a yellow dust called pollen. For fruit to grow, pollen needs to move from one flower to another. Insects move the pollen as they feed.

The apples ripen

During the summer, the apples get bigger and bigger. By autumn, they are ripe.

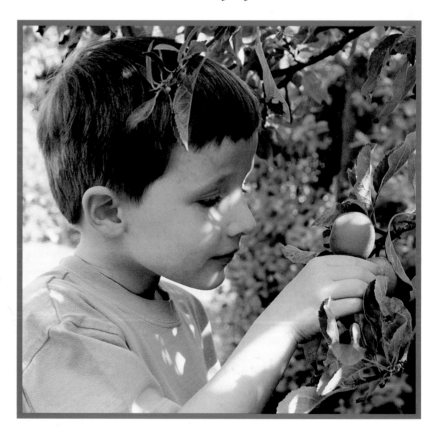

▶ *Young apples are small and hard.*

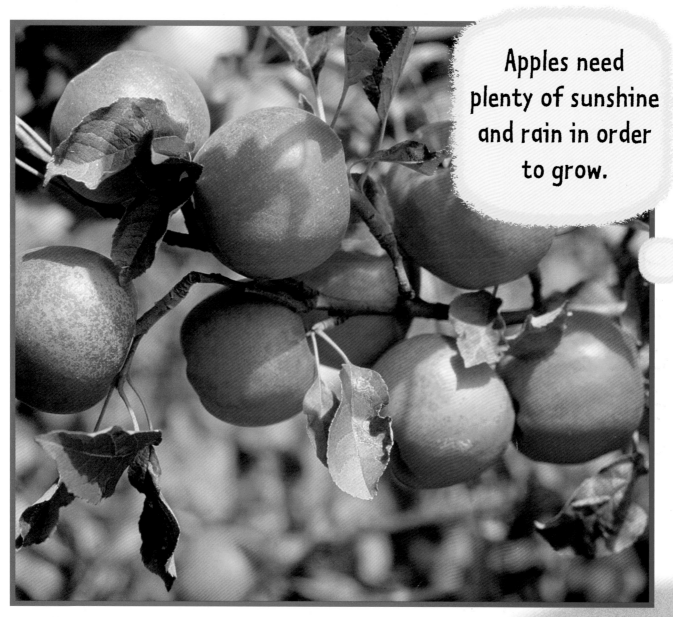

Apples need plenty of sunshine and rain in order to grow.

▲ *Some apples change colour as they get ripe.*

From orchard to shop

Ripe apples are picked and put into boxes. Then they are taken to markets and shops.

▶ *The apples are picked by hand.*

We can buy many different kinds of apples at the shops.

Apples have to be picked very carefully. What happens to an apple if you bump it or drop it?

Apple juice

Some apples are used to make apple juice. Machines crush the apples and press out the juice.

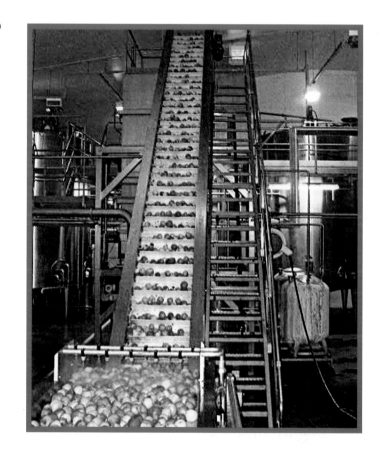

▶ *These apples are going into the apple press, where they will be made into juice.*

Apple juice is sold in bottles and cartons.

It takes two whole apples to make a glass of juice.

pure
apple
juice

pure
apple
juice

19

Cooking with apples

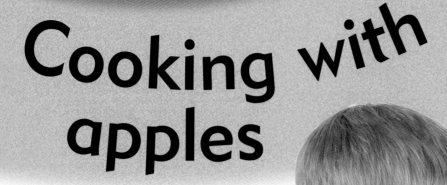

We often eat apples raw. We can also cook them in different ways.

What is your favourite apple treat?

Apples make delicious pies and puddings.

I know that...

1 Apples are a kind of fruit.

2 Apples are good for our bodies.

3 An apple has a stalk, peel, flesh, a core and seeds.

4 Apples are the fruit of the apple tree.

5 Apple trees grow in orchards.

6 In spring, apple trees are covered in blossom.

7 Apples grow in summer. By autumn, they are ripe.

8 Apples are picked when they are ripe. They are sold in shops and markets.

9 Apples are used to make apple juice.

10 We can cook apples in many different ways.

Index

About this book

I Know That! is designed to introduce children to the process of gathering information and using reference books, one of the key skills needed to begin more formal learning at school. For this reason, each book's structure reflects the information books children will use later in their learning career – with key information in the main text and additional facts and ideas in the captions. The panels give an opportunity for further activities, ideas or discussions. The contents page and index are helpful reference guides.

The language is carefully chosen to be accessible to children just beginning to read. Illustrations support the text but also give information in their own right; active consideration and discussion of images is another key referencing skill. The main aim of the series is to build confidence – showing children how much they already know and giving them the ability to gather new information for themselves. With this in mind, the *I know that...* section at the end of the book is a simple way for children to revisit what they already know as well as what they have learnt from reading the book.